The Town of Torper
and the
Very Vulgar Day Lily

A Cautionary Tale

By Ellen Anne Eddy

This little story is a cautionary tale, not necessarily true but full of truth. Any resemblance to people living or dead is completely coincidental.

Wars of all sorts have unexpected outcomes. Often our victories cost more than the world can afford. In this small space, no one's loss is just theirs. A heavy handed win can be the first shot of the next war.

We live gently on this planet together, flora and fauna. Harmony, like a well planted garden, is hard fought for and worth gold.

Ellen Anne Eddy

Acknowledgements

My thanks to Art Elwood, Sherril Newman, Rita and Wade Newman, Big Mike and Little Mike, and to Good Folk everywhere.

Ellen Anne Eddy's quilts, Fall Confetti, Day Lily Dance and Butterfly Garden have been used as illustrations for this book. All rights reserved. More of her works and information about classes are available at www.ellenanneddy.com.

For Ray Dear and Mary, both people who have loved gardens, people and growth more than order.

The Town of Torper and the Very Vulgar Day lily
By Ellen Anne Eddy
Copyright 2011
978-0-9822901-5-6

Thread Magic Studio Press
125 Franklin Street
Porter, IN 46304
219-921-0885
www.ellenanneddy.com

The perfect book for garden, schools, guild and library fundraising. Available at special discount prices for group sales.

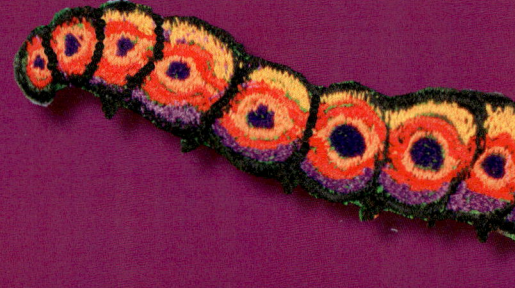

The Town of Torper

The town of Torper was an imaginary place. Like most small towns, it ran in pathways unchanged by time. So it was also timeless. This little story could have happened 50 years ago and may happen again in 55 years from now. The human heart is mostly unchanged and uncharted.

Torper had its standards. In the matter of small spaces everywhere there were arbiters of good taste. They carefully expressed their opinions to all of us less tasteful mortals lest we fall from grace and plant something inappropriate in the garden.

In the tasteful town of Torper an evil event was about to happen. Torper was about to be invaded. Not by rats or mice, not by politicians (we already had a surfeit of those), or mosquitoes, nothing new. No. It's to be invaded by day lilies.

Now in this pillar of good taste and elegant small town chic, most people bought their garden supplies at the Mallmart. Everyone went there. Where else would one go? They returned with the same lawn chairs, grass seed, and ornaments. No vulgar plants were allowed.

The Root of the Matter

The day lily arrived in a bucket, several weeks after the woman moved in. It was a gift from a friend. She planted it in the the parkway, a strip between the lawn and the road, to brighten up the place, and pretty much forgot it.

The day lily, though clearly a weedy girl was a perennial. So the perennial rules applied. First year, sleep. Second year creep. Third year leap. So she snuggled into the soil of the parkway, quietly waiting, growing new roots.

She wasn't hiding. Honest. She just had other things on her mind.

It was a whole year later when she started to think about flowering.

Day Lily Adolescent Angst

Her second year the day lily just couldn't be as discreet. It just didn't work. For one thing, she was bigger. And out of no where this big green shoot sprouted, that was in no way discreet. Blessedly it was still green.

But she found herself swaying with the breeze, aware that she was more like a prairie grass than like many impatients and marigolds around her. Her roots soaked up the rain. Her leaves basked in the sun. As it got warmer and sweeter outside, she formed a huge bud. The sun and wind and rain did their work. When the bud opened, God help us all, it was orange!

Torper Reacts

The first people to notice the day lily of course were not people. People are busy creatures, with no time for flowers.

But the rest of Torper definitely noticed. The lady bugs in the garden saw she had aphids on her, and graciously ate them. A praying mantis found her leaves a wonderful place to hide in and wait. Three dogs in the neighborhood sprinkled a bit to offer her some fertilizer. The cats found her leaves made a wonderful jungle for a nap.

The birds had a bird's eye view. They flew over her amazing orange bloom and were so astonished that their mouths fell open. Several dropped the seeds they were carrying home from their wandering. They were so amazed they couldn't contain themselves. They dropped little bird droppings right next to the lily. So seeds of all kinds were sowed around. All kinds of wonderful wild weeds moved in.

The Politics of Plants and People

By now our day lily was out. Very out. And out loud as well. As the prairie grasses grew around her, she found herself growing slightly into the side walk area. Many people walked by slowly, taking in the beauty of the wild. They touched her petals and were touched by her beauty. But not everyone felt that way.

Riley was a woman in the neighborhood with the best Mallmart yard. She had precisely the blandest colored, least obtrusive green plants. She had the official yard ornaments available only at Mallmart. One day Riley walked by and accidentally brushed against the lily.

She was terrified! It was Orange! It was in the walk way! It was, most of all, out of her control.

She screamed," It touched me! I've been attacked! Assaulted!" Yelling through the neighborhood, she rushed into the safety of her home. Even large quantities of cigarettes and adult beverages failed to restore her calm.

Drama Trauma

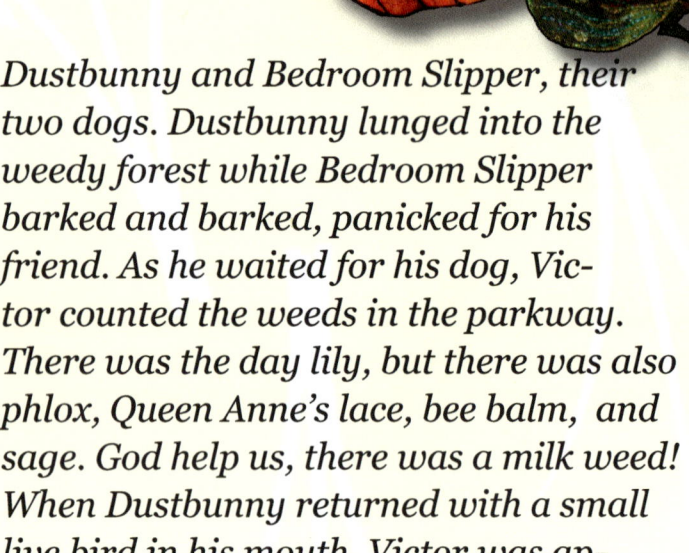

When Riley's husband Victor got home that night he found her stretched out on the couch, still traumatized.

"What happened?" he asked as he fanned her forehead.

"I was assaulted by a day lily!"

Victor above all, loved his wife but he also valued a peaceful life. "Really? A day lily?"

"Yes! It climbed right up my leg!"

"Oh, dear!"

"It curled up my leg!

"Oh, dear!"

"It almost reached my panties!"

"Oh, dear!"

"It was ORANGE!"

"Oh, dear!"

Clearly something must be done.

Now in the town of Torper there were no laws exactly against day lilies. Good taste stood its stead against any large orange flower, but there wasn't any exact rule against them. But Riley knew she was not safe until the day lily and its weedy friends were gone.

She sent Victor out to look. He brought Dustbunny and Bedroom Slipper, their two dogs. Dustbunny lunged into the weedy forest while Bedroom Slipper barked and barked, panicked for his friend. As he waited for his dog, Victor counted the weeds in the parkway. There was the day lily, but there was also phlox, Queen Anne's lace, bee balm, and sage. God help us, there was a milk weed! When Dustbunny returned with a small live bird in his mouth, Victor was appalled. Well, so was the bird.

He made Dustbunny drop the bird and dragged both dogs inside. He told his wife, "Well, of course, we'll have to do something. It clearly isn't safe."

So they went about deciding how to defend against the menace of day lilies.

The Building Inspector of Torper

The building inspector of Torper was a man with many hats. He inspected buildings of course, but he also found lost dogs, stopped nasty arguments, listened a great deal to all kinds of nonsense and knew how to nod just as if he'd agreed even when he was nodding off. He could also tap dance like a fiend.

Every morning he would look in the mirror, smile a crooked smile, and mentally put on his black cowboy hat and gun belt, just to be safe. Point of fact, it was all a disguise. He was a man who appreciated law, good sense and general decency, in that order.

The morning Riley called him, there was not enough coffee in the universe or anywhere else for what needed to happen next.

"She has a day lily in her parkway! Right next to a milk weed! My dog found a bird in there! There have to be rats and moles and mosquitoes and probably poisonous snakes as well! Make her dig it up."

Although there wasn't enough coffee, he drank all he could find and mustered up his answer.

"I'll go out and take a look." He peered in the mirror, checked the tilt of his imaginary hat, and swaggered out to look at the crime scene.

Criminal Gardening

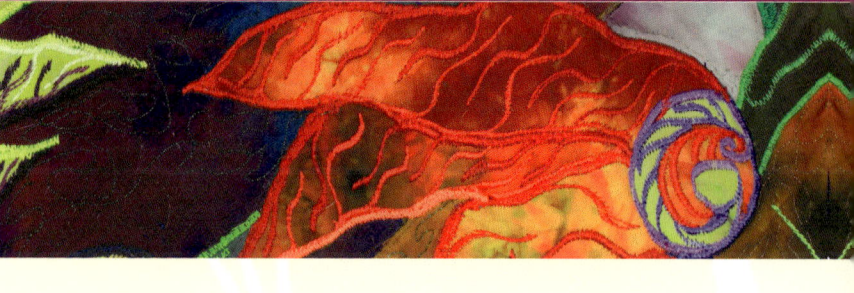

When the building inspector arrived, Riley was sitting on her porch soaking up cigarette smoke and coffee in about the same amounts. He got out of his car and looked at the offending strip of garden.

It was a section of prairie flowers and day lilies, with butterflies soaring over their heads. It was also definitely leaning into the walkway.

Riley stood at her part of the sidewalk, unwilling to go closer.

"Do you see what I mean? Anything could be in there. Mice. rats, vipers…."

The inspector noticed a Bedroom Slipper size dog poop and said, "I see what you mean."

She then turned to the rest of the woman's yard. It was full of flowers and bushes. Weeds. Trees. In fact, it had no grass at all. "Surely, she's committing a crime here. It's not safe. It's not sanitary. Can't we make her just plant a lawn like everyone else? She even has mint in back, growing wild."

He shook his head and said, "Well there are plants on the parkway."

Riley went back inside, sure she'd made her point.

The building inspector went back to the station, had three more cups of coffee and prepared himself for the next phone call.

Best Efforts Failed

The building inspector picked up his phone and his courage. Experience had taught him that telling someone to dig out their garden was something akin to explaining to a mother bear why you wanted to take her baby out of the den.

No matter what you did, no one was going to be happy after that. What you really were hoping for was that no one would end up dead.

As it is, the lady who owned the garden blissfully missed the punch line entirely. "I can cut it back. Sure. Not a problem."

She went out, cut out around 22 wheel barrows of foliage and thought it a job well done. Three weeks and a hard rain later, it looked exactly as it had before.

Riley called back to say she'd been accosted by something purple and pokey. Something had to be done.

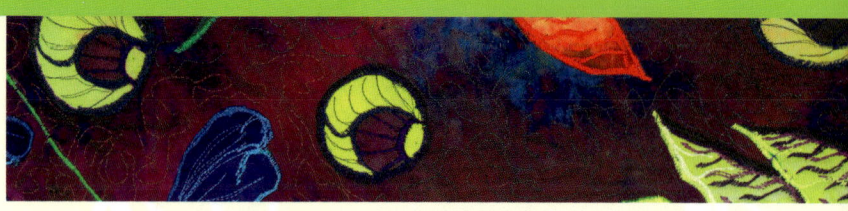

Old Hyperion

The poor day lily also missed the punch line, being very inexperienced with small town politics. But she had caught on that a lot of folk were walking up, looking at her and screaming a lot. That was hard to miss. In her heart it hurt her feelings. She was a simple lovely lily. No pretensions. No aspirations. Just the sweet life of rain and sun and wind. How could everyone be so upset?

Now the rest of the yard past the park way was also full of plant life. It included huge flowering shrubs, roses, lilacs, smoke trees, hostas, hydrangeas, and a huge weeping juniper. A good three dozen weeds nestled safely in between. So it was no surprise that when she looked back into the yard, she saw a plant she'd not noticed before.

He was shorter than her. And yellow. But he was a day lily too.

He smiled at her. "Well, little girl, you've got yourself in some trouble."

She was so stunned she said nothing. Finally she asked him, "Why aren't you orange too?"

He said, "I was designed that way. They featured me as the most important garden plant of 1927."

"Is that how old you are?, she choked.

"In a way. I've been passed down through this family for three generations. Every time the family has moved it took part of me along and planted me in their yard. I'm a Hyperion."

"That sounds awfully elevated. You're just yellow."

"But I bloom more than once a year and back then, yellow was sort of special. Now I'm a part of the family, and they'd never consider leaving me behind."

"What is going on here? There are people incredibly upset and they seem to be upset with me."

"That's a perception. You're the target. You're not the cause."

Hyperion closed his eyes and took a breath.

"There are only two reactions people are capable of. Fear and love. They do a lot of things, but they're all one or the other, sometimes just dressed up funny."

He began to explain the care and feeding of upset humans.

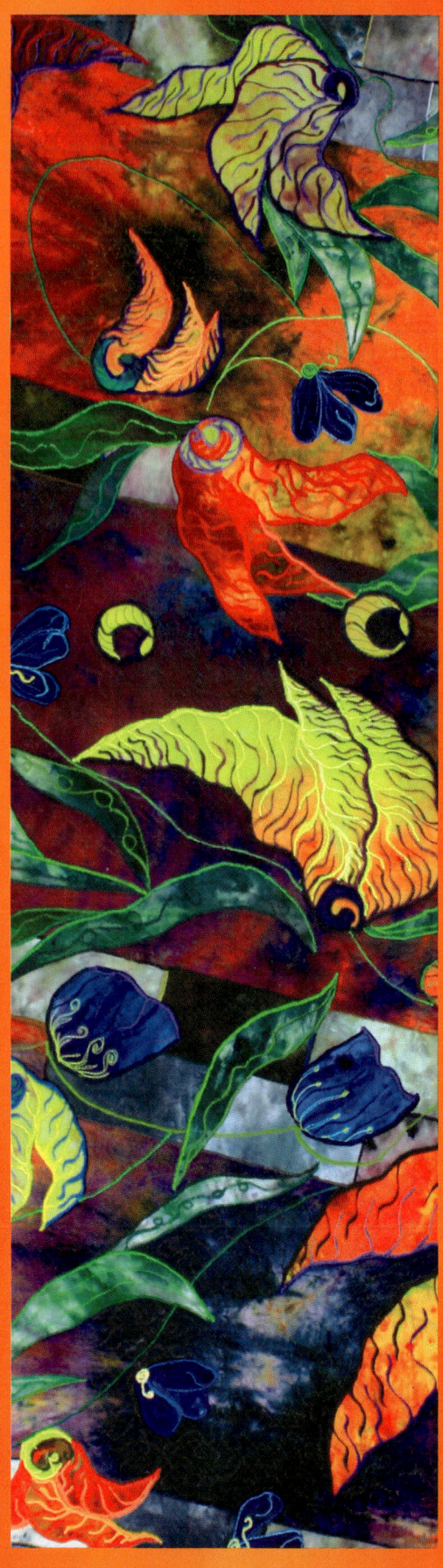

The Distraught and Distressed

Hyperion had seen it all. He'd moved with his family for over 80 years through different locations. He'd had a full view of human interaction in gardens. But he'd seen gardens planted in and dug up, and he knew what was on the horizon. Put simply, frightened people brought out hoes and got scary, without much warning. He tried to prepare her for what was coming.

"Their fear is their fear. You can't reach past it or change it or turn it aside. But you can wait for love to come through. If you can hold on long enough, love always comes through."

"Hearts and flowers? Birds and bees?" She asked.

"Heavens, no. Care and support, a place to stand, people to stand behind you. An acknowledgement of your place in the world. Given time, that always comes. And help unexpected. Hearts and flowers are a pale version of love. They're symbols, not facts or actions. They're nouns, not verbs"

She turned her head. She'd heard as much as she could. He stretched roots in the soil and waited.

The Good Folk

BACK TO THE BUILDING INSPECTOR:

He'd seen garden wars before. They were nasty. Like all wars, the outcome was not about justice. It's not necessarily true that might makes right or that the just prevail. It was more a matter of who was craziest. The garden strip was an indication of a person who lived pretty close to the edge of that. It was pretty wild. But anyone who thought it contained vipers was probably barking nuts. And the day lily's garden strip was undeniably beautiful. There was something wrong in simply destroying it.

He knew when he was out of his depths. He picked up his phone and called for help.

Now all throughout history there have been people who have a special connection with the land. And who are larger than life. The Irish call them the fairies. Every culture has some version. Dressing them up in cute clothes and little wings is merely a disguise. They live for and by the land and nothing else really matters to them. They are also called the Good Folk, but not because all they do is good. It is in an effort to not annoy them, which is always a bad idea.

The stories are all the same in this regard. YOU DO NOT MESS WITH THE FAIRIES.

Being from a watered down technological society, he even knew a phone number that would connect him. He made that call, and the earth began slowly and quietly to shift in another direction.

Hyperion felt it in his roots, and breathed easier. There would be help.

The day lily didn't know what she was feeling, but something had changed.

The woman with the garden sighed and rolled over and couldn't quite remember her dream the next morning.

Riley woke up sure that rats and snakes were under her front porch.

Bedroom Slipper cocked his head and looked out the window and started to bark at what was, apparently, nothing.

And the Town of Torper prepared for battle with the might of Vulgar Day lilies.

The Forces Gather

How does a day lily fight? It's a moot point. A day lily simply isn't equipped. Fighting isn't what they do. They might be aggressive in their desire for water, sun and wind, but they don't duke it out with each other. People work differently. Fighting is simply what people do when all other options (like rational thought, arbitration, and courtesy) have disappeared. Most fights go on long before battle and end years later. Wars are simply a cathartic moment when somebody has a temper tantrum. The rest of it blows cold and hot at different moments, but the momentum is still there.

Now there is a place where a day lily can stand. Her fight is simply her presence. Are you stronger in a world with or without day lilies? It's as simple as that.

Now people fight. Long before, during and after battles, it's how they hold their own. Tooth, claw, complaint and summons. Usually when they're terrified.

Hard words and pointy objects are all the product of fear dressed up funny. Except that it's hardly humorous.

The Good Folk are something else. They fight. But like all survivors, they change the rules. You believe you've won and you've won ashes. You believe you've lost but things are not what you think. Check your assumptions. You might want to check them at the door. Your world as you know it is about to change.

The building inspector, neither fish nor fowl, stood on the sidelines, his invisible pistols by his side in case there was need. He wasn't permitted to take sides. Of course by calling in The Good Folk, he knew in the end, he wouldn't have to.

D-Day

The law is always the law which is always the law. As always, seen through a million different eyes, it comes out differently each time. But the basics stay constant. Torper had declared that there should be no plants larger than four inches tall in the parkway. So a day of demolition was inevitable.

The Good Folk made their plans and arrived. When the truck pulled up, Riley was absolutely beside herself with joy!

Would they dig up the strip? Would they dig up all the trees? The milkweed? Would they finally cut it all down? She could have a neighborhood safe for all Mallmart Lawns and their owners. Most of all, she had made it happen. She glowed with power and pride.

The Good Folk started to dig, and clip, cut and chop. The day lily felt herself dug up and lifted out by not unkindly hands. It was terrifying. She was joined by many other lilies as well as the other prairie grasses, tucked in pots or in the pile on the truck. Soon there was nothing but a strip of dead dry earth.

Then an odd thing happened. They stopped cutting. Something had gone terribly wrong.

Riley's heart skipped. She ran out. She stared. She certainly couldn't go to the woman and ask. That was direct conflict, far too scary.

So she spoke to one of the Folk. "Aren't you going to cut down that tree?"

"No. Why?"

"But aren't you going to cut down that bush?"

"No. Why?"

"Aren't you going to take out that milkweed?"

"No. Why?"

This was not working right.

She retreated into the house and fortified herself with more adult beverages and a chimney's worth of cigarette smoke.

Then she called the building inspector. "They're not cutting everything down. I demand you come down and talk to them." Invisible hat and gun belt in hand, he drove down.

Yours, Mine, and Not Yours

A PRIMER IN OWNERSHIP:

Riley was desperate to notice that there were still large plants in the woman's yard, that might someday lean over her Mallmart lawn. After getting no help from the Good Folk who suggested she sit down and rest before she had a heart attack, she called the building inspector.

As he arrived, she rushed up. "They won't cut down the lilac!"

"Is it in the parkway?"

"Well, no, but it's near my yard. They won't cut down the smoke tree!"

"Is it in the parkway?"

"Well, no but it's near my gutter. They won't cut down the lilac!"

This went on for some while. He took her gently by the shoulders and turned her to the very dead mud pit of the parkway. "She dug up her parkway. What do you want?"

"A safe place for tasteful lawns that everyone mows on time! Isn't that what everyone wants?"

"You'll have to be satisfied with your achievement. The parkway, rain garden and the day lily are gone." He tipped his invisible hat, and went off to have a bath. It had been a rough day in law enforcement.

She stared at the mud pit and began to feel better. This was a test of her power, her skill, her acknowledged taste and good sense. Dustbunny left a small poop on the mud pit, and she gathered him in and went inside to plan her next campaign. Perhaps she could kill off all the mint with Roundup while no one was looking.

Three streets down, the Good Folk had stopped their truck and a crowd had gathered. "Would you like a day lily?" one of them shouted.

The crowd moved closer. They'd never seen colors like this. One little boy said "Mom, can I have one?" She indulged her child. They went home with three.

It broke the dam. One by one, the people of Torper took arm loads of lilies, phlox and bee balm home and tucked them into their garden beds. The day lily smiled, safe in the boy's yard. Other plants stretched their roots into the dirt. A soft rain began to fall and soak the new turned soil.

The Need For Sunglasses

The next morning, Riley woke with a lighter heart. This was just a beginning. Look at all the good she'd done for little Torper. Torper needed someone with excellent taste and a talent for ducking confrontation. Perhaps she'd run for town council.

She and her dogs walked out to look at the mud pit. There it was, bare, stark and completely colorless. She smiled broadly. Then she looked up.

Across the street from her was the day lily. It winked at her. It was not in the parkway. It was safely in the neighbor's garden bed. It was blazingly orange.

Surely not. Surely not. No. She turned. The next house had bee balm in flagrant red. The house after that an indecent purple phlox. As she walked past house after house, all kinds of garden beds had brilliantly colored flowers. There were mounds of incredibly vulgar, blatantly orange day lilies.

Victor found her two hours later, sobbing on the steps of their house. He got her into the house, put a cold cloth over her eyes and closed the blinds. Later, he went out to buy her some dark sunglasses.

Manicured Lawns

The lady took a fair sampling of her dug up bed, including a root of the day lily and put it safely in a bed around her parking lot. Soon shoots greened up and started to bloom.

The rest of Torper found itself in love with color. They went looking for wild plants, prairie grasses, odd native offerings that had wonderful, tall brave plumages. It was very arty, very wild and ablaze with color.

Riley did not fare so well. Her head hurt all the time. Any time she needed to leave the house she put on dark glasses so her eyes didn't hurt. She threw crockery. She yelled a lot. Victor took to mowing the lawn four times a week.

Within several weeks, it was clear that that she was not coping.

Victor made some calls. There were sad but necessary conversations.

Several days later a quiet ambulance pulled up to the house. The men were very gentle with her. "You just need a rest. The lawns at Quiet More are meticulously groomed. You'll love it there." They led her stumbling into the van. The breeze made the day lilies seem to wave goodbye.

Dreams and Defeats

Victor went back to the house. He was devastated by his wife's breakdown. He, too, loathed and hated any yard out of control. He hated weeds, but most of all he hated trees. They dropped things in his gutter. He loathed the smoke bush because it came near his gutter. He hated the maple because it had seeds in spring and leaves in the fall and both went in his gutter. He despised the weeping juniper because it blocked his view of his neighbors window and he couldn't see in. He hated any tree that might someday grow over his yard. His life was a struggle against nature raw and wild in the way of his lawn mower. He'd already hacked up the azalea bush that was near his yard. It interfered with his mowing. The struggle to keep his lawn perfectly mowed and his gutters perfectly clean was more than the man could bear. How could you possibly add trees and bushes without pushing him past his edge?

The neighbor woman put up a fence. This was very shocking because it went up on the property line. He had no idea he had that little property on that side of the house. The fence left about a foot and a half of space for his yard. The plants he had been complaining about were strictly in her yard. Now he would have to ask permission to clean his gutters because

the ladder would have to go in her yard.

His lawn mower didn't fit through the passage. He went over and told the neighbor lady she had to cut down the trees and take down the fence. They were a menace and a nuisance.

He called the building inspector. When the building inspector arrived, he showed Victor where the surveying pin was, explained again that the things that weren't in his yard weren't in his control and told him no. When the lady told him no, Victor stomped off in his fury.

Much later that night he slept. And he dreamed. He was in his yard. But he was lying in it. Face up. He couldn't move. He saw something push through his fence. It was the trees. They drooped over the top. They pushed through the cracks. The big maple stepped delicately over the fence and leaned over to him. He was terrified. Leaves brushed his face.

"Breathe," she said. "You know you can't breathe without us. You hate the mess and the fuss, the branches and the overgrowth, but we make the very air you breathe. Everyone breathes. Even you."

The azalea ducked through the opening in the fence. "Breathe," she said. "Smell that wonderful fragrance. We frighten you and you see us as being more work, but we add the scents and sights that make the world more lovely and whole. Even you."

The day lily bent through the opening and touched his cheek. He flinched.

"Breathe." She said." I know you're afraid of bugs, and rats and me. But we're part of the food cycle. Food doesn't come from the grocery store. Everyone eats, even you."

Victor woke wet and miserable to the sound of a branch tapping at his window.

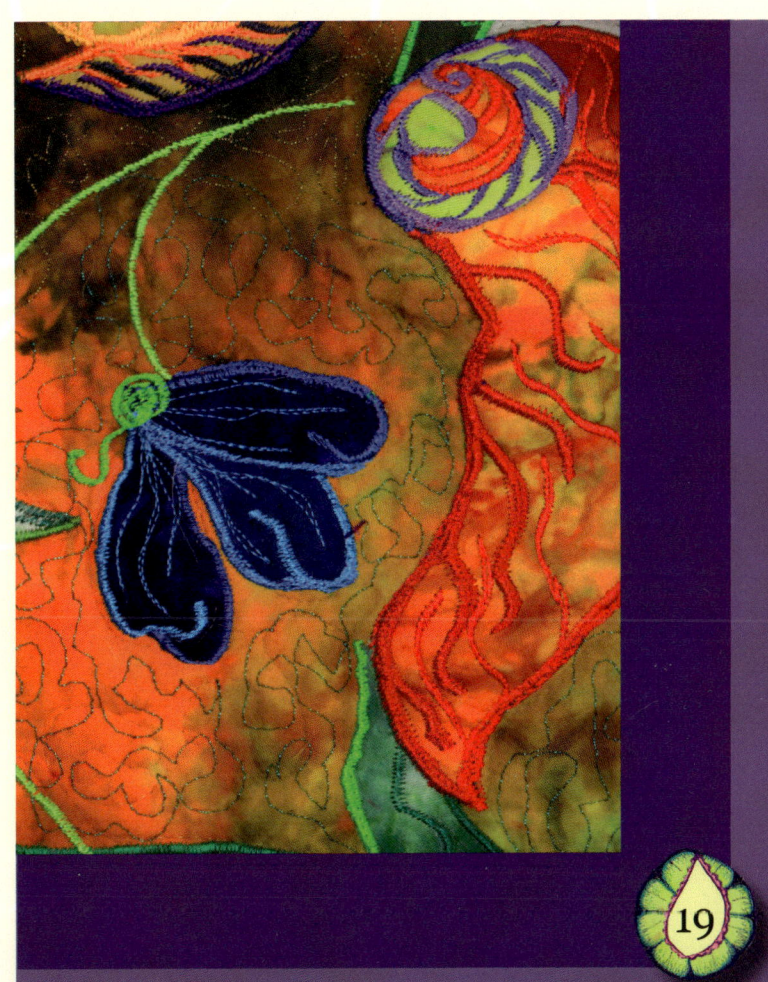

The Rest of Life

Victor stumbled down the stairs. Bedroom Slipper and Dustbunny circled at his feet. He fed them each a cookie.

Over the next of couple weeks he needed to hunt a home for them in a gated community with some truly strict garden standards. Far away from wild trees. Far away from bushes. Far away from beauty, breath, scent and blossom. There are worlds of nothing but concrete. One man's heaven is another's hell. You can find them both, if you try.

You may believe you've won when you've won ashes. You may believe you've lost, but things are not what you think. Check your assumptions, somewhere near the door. Your world as you know it has changed.

Our day lily and her many daughters wave over the town of Torper, proud of their orange heritage, loved for who they are. A rainbow of flowers grow beside them. The sun, the wind and the rain bless them all. And the town of Torper basks in the glow.

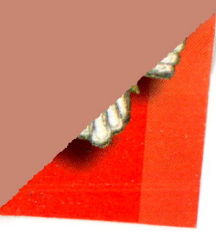

LaVergne, TN USA
28 February 2011
218212LV00005B